Q.

"Grief – It's NOT Supposed to be OK!"

A Companion/Standalone Workbook, Journal and Self-Care Guide.

By Ron Skinner and Jeff Kirk

Contents

Copyright

ABOUT THIS WORKBOOK

This workbook can be used with the book "Grief-It's NOT Supposed To Be OK!" Or as a standalone prompted guide to examine and better understand your grief. Ideal: as a companion to the book, it will help you take the wealth of information presented in the book and internalizing it as is applies to your grief. You are guided by both thought-provoking questions and reminders of the information in the book. Ample room throughout this workbook allows you to expound upon the book and note any additional thoughts you may have as you go through the workbook.

This workbook is an excellent way to collect your thoughts about your grief. Writing your thoughts and feelings provides a needed avenue for understanding what you are going through. Follow along with chapter by chapter prompts in the workbook as you read "Grief - It's NOT Supposed To Be OK!" You may be surprised by how much progress you have made on your journey with grief.

Quick access to the book is available at the link below. Enter the link or use your smartphone camera to scan the QRC.

https://amazon.com/dp/B09SL7MYW5

Preface (Page 15)

Does your loss seem to be the same for you as it is for others around you? Take a moment to explain.

How has your life changed?

Your Thoughts:

Introduction (Page 19)

Why does your relationship with the one you lost seem to change your grief?

My Thoughts:

List one or more ways that you have dealt with your loss:

Has your grief affected your relationship with others around you?

List one or two people who care about and you know to be levelheaded who might come alongside you and help you

NAME	PHONE NUMBER

Understanding There Is No Wrong Way to Grieve (page 25)

Take a few minutes to think about all the emotions that have come to the surface as you grieve and jot them down below. After you record each of your feelings, think about why you may have such feelings and write it down below your emotion:

I feel:
Because:
I feel:
Because:
I feel:
Because:
I feel:
Because:

I feel:
Because:
I feel:
Because:
I feel:
Because:
I feel:
Because:
I feel:
Because:
I feel:
Because:
I feel:
Because:
I feel:
Because:

Understanding That Your Grief Is Unique (page 27)

Can you list a few reasons that your grief differs from others?

My Thoughts:

Understanding Grief Has No Time Limit (page 29)

Elisabeth Kubler-Ross wrote a book titled "On Death and Dying", in it she wrote that "the reality is that you will grieve forever."

Do you believe you will ever stop grieving completely for the one you lost? Please explain:

What do you think the relationship between love and grief is?

My Thoughts:

Stages…. Really? (page 31)

The "Five Stages" theorized by Kubler-Ross in her 1969 book were never intended to be a lineal roadmap for our grief

Has your grief journey followed any logical or lineal progression through "The Five Stages of Grief"?

List the 5 Stages of Grief as expressed by Kubler-Ross:

1.
2.
3.
4.
5.

Have you experienced these stages in a certain order?

Have you found yourself in any of these stages more than once? Provide details.

Do you think your journey is following any logical or lineal progression through "The Five Stages of Grief"?

Write down your unique journey through grief stages.

If you were pressed to pick a stage of grief you are in right now, what stage or stages would you choose? (If more than one stage, list multiple stages)

Additional Notes:

So, How Do We Cope? (page 41)

What are your greatest emotional needs when struck with grief?

If you are honest with yourself, could you say that these needs are being met?

List ways these emotional needs can be met.

List some of the physical symptoms that you are more susceptible to if your needs are not met:

Signs of Complicated Grief (page 49)

In your own words, describe complicated grief:

List at least 4 of the 8 Symptoms of Complicate Grief referenced.

1)	
2)	
3)	
4)	
5)	
6)	
7)	
8)	

If, after reviewing, you believe you may suffer from complicated grief, then seek help. It is **NOT** a sign of weakness to seek help. There are resources listed in the accompanying book on page 55, and here on page 22.

Your Thoughts:

Major or Clinical Depression (page 51)

Are grief and depression the same thing? Explain briefly:

List one major difference that can help you determine if you are grieving or if you are depressed:

List at least two symptoms in each category below that you may experience with depression that would not typically accompany grief:

FEELINGS	THOUGHTS	PHYSICAL

My Thoughts:

When To Get Help (page 53)

If you have the book, review pages 53 and 54 of "Grief - It's NOT Supposed To Be OK!" Please, **DO NOT** put off getting help if you are experiencing the symptoms listed.

It is far braver (and more loving to those who you care about) to seek help than to suffer in silence. Resources to help are at your fingertips and are so important that we have listed them here on page 22, as well as the accompanying book.

We feel that the early identification is so important; we are including a quick link to those pages, for those without the book.

If you need help, please talk to someone.

Use the QRC

We all need help sometimes. Reach out when you need to!

Emergency Resources Nationally:
Dial 911

Crisis Services:
24/7 Crisis Hotline: National Suicide Prevention Lifeline Network
www.suicidepreventionlifeline.org

National Suicide Lifeline:
(800) 273-TALK (8255) Veterans press 1

Crisis Text Line:
Text TALK to 741-741 to text with a trained crisis counselor from the Crisis Text Line for free, 24 / 7

American Foundation for Suicide Prevention:
(800) 333-2377

Veterans
send a text to 82825

American Foundation for Suicide Prevention
www.afsp.org

My Thoughts:

What Coping Does Not Mean (page 57)

Does Coping always mean "Being Strong"?

Could there be times during your grief when showing emotions might help both you and those around you? Briefly explain.

List Different ways that you have expressed your grief: (*hint: it does not have to be the way others think it should be. If it works for you, that's all that matters.)

Does "Coping" mean you are done grieving? Explain.

Finding Your Way Now (page 59)

There are so many details to attend to when we lose a loved one. Don't forget about you.

What is one of the first things that you must do for yourself?

Grief can affect mind, body, and soul. Briefly list some of the physical reactions you have gone through.

Have you been affected spiritually? Take a moment to write any changes in your faith or beliefs that your loss may have influenced.

Recognizing what you are going through and labeling it makes it less mysterious and scary.

Detail the emotional reactions involved in your grief.

Have you experienced any cognitive reactions to your loss? If so, list them here.

How have you behaved differently towards others or in your thoughts or actions?

Don't Forget That Your Children are Grieving Too (page 67)

After reading "Grief - It's NOT Supposed To Be OK!", many find that their children's needs during this time have not been fully met. Examine your own journey with grief and jot down the times when you could have been more helpful to them.

Is there anything you could say or do now that might help your children?

Do your kids need you to "be strong" so that they know everything is OK? (Hint: everything is NOT Ok!) What do your children need from you as they grieve?

Do you feel it is OK for your children to see you sad, even crying about your loss sometimes? Explain.

My Thoughts.

What About You? (page 71)

Are you taking the time you need for yourself? Describe
what you are doing for your own wellbeing during this time:

What is your "place of escape"? (Hint: this may or not be a
physical place. It could be an activity that simply allows
your mind to rest and recoup):

What specific things are you consciously doing to take
care of your body right now?

My thoughts:

Outward Struggles of Grief (page 77)

You may be left with the responsibility of going through your loved one's possessions. The how, when, where, and even to whom may fall upon you now.

How you will handle this?

How does it make you feel when you see and talk to people who remind you of your loss?

Have you ever been "triggered" by someone (even a total stranger) who instantly reminded you of your loved one causing unexpected emotions?

Can you briefly explain that experience, including why they reminded you of your loss?

Special occasions, whether it be holidays, anniversaries, birthdays, or other times, can be very difficult. If you have such times throughout the year, list those special times and what you can do to make it a little easier for yourself:

Inward Struggles of Grief (page 83)

List some ways the loss of your loved one has created struggles for you.

You may have specific feelings after your loss that you don't understand. Write your feelings and why you may have them. (Remember, there are no wrong feelings)

Why do we often punish ourselves or have misplaced guilt?

How can you work through these feelings?

My Thoughts:

Tears and Strength (page 99)

Is there a right or wrong way for you to grieve your loss?

What does your grief look like?

Have those around misunderstood your reactions to grief? List examples:

Isolation and Loneliness (page 101)

Have you found you sometimes want to be alone in your grief?

Examine yourself and jot down why you feel this way:

Have you experienced social or emotional isolation?

Why?

Do you feel lonely?

List some ways you can combat loneliness and isolation:

Make a brief plan detailing at least 3 specific things you can do to overcome loneliness and isolation:

1

2

3

The Fallacy of Closure (page 109)

Why can we never truly have closure with grief?

Why is expecting closure unrealistic?

How is our grief like pealing back the layers of an onion?

My Thoughts:

Moving on in Your Grief (page 113)

What does "moving on in your grief" mean to you?

Explain why others seem so intent that you should "move on."

Explain why moving on does not mean we forget or that our grief has ended:

Give an example in your life where the adage "Time Heals all Wounds" simply was not true.

List at least 3 things you can do as you move forward with your grief:

My Thoughts:

Continuing the Race (page 121)

"Well, everyone can master a grief but he that has it"

-William Shakespeare

How can we view the unwelcome intrusions in our life, often when we least expect them? (i.e. the outburst of tears or anger that come from some "trigger")

List the reason (s) that you have found yourself not engaging in life because of your grief (i.e., I don't want to go out to lunch with the girls because I know they will talk about their kids, and it hurts too much):

Why should you engage, even if you don't want to?

Take the time to complete this exercise to help you "Get Back in the Saddle"

Step One:

List below everything you do in the day hour by hour, line by line, and how long you take to do it.

Step Two:

Look at your list. Should you be doing more? Maybe you should do less? Now review your list closely and highlight each activity:
a) Emotionally draining activities - red
b) Things you are doing out of avoidance or worry - pink
c) Activities involving self-care, positivity, and coping - green

Step Three:

List below all the activities you used to enjoy or were meaningful to you that you aren't doing anymore.

Step Four:

1) Look at each red activity and decide if it **MUST** be in your schedule.
   a) Keep only those red activities. Throw out any other red activities.
2) Remove all pink activities that are not helping you in your grief. Be brutally honest with yourself.
3) All green activities stay.
4) Take some time and add any additional green activities you can think of.
5) Finally, review both lists (Step One and Step Three) carefully and make a new schedule for yourself.
   a) This may require a notebook or day-planner, as days vary.
6) Follow your new schedule.

What impact has your new schedule had on your daily life?

Are there ways you can continue to improve on this new schedule with time?

List at least three things you can do to help deal with the changes in your life:

My Thoughts:

People Sometimes say the Most Hurtful Things (page 143)

Write down the foolish or hurtful things people have said to you while grieving:

_____
_____
_____
_____
_____
_____
_____
_____
_____
_____

What do you believe is the best way to deal with their painful words?

_____
_____
_____
_____
_____
_____
_____
_____
_____

Recall a time in your own life when words slipped from your mouth that you now wish you could take back.

List at least 4 "safe" things you can say to others when they are grieving.

Specific Relational and Conditional Losses (page 149)

Losing a spouse is like losing a part of yourself. Your ever-present companion and friend. Take a minute and make a mental inventory of the most unexpected things that you miss about your spouse.

What do you miss the most?

My Thoughts:

All death is tragic, and all grief is unique, but losing a child seems to bring a type of grief like no other.

Why is the loss of a child so devastating?

When a precious human life is lost through miscarriage or stillbirth, the pain, suffering and grief that ensues are just as severe. Why do these grieving parents not seem to get the same empathy and understanding?

Studies show that between 12% and 16% of divorces involve the death of a child.

How can we explain such a tragic statistic?

Death of a child at any age is beyond comprehension to those who haven't been through it. Please list a few things that might help as you carry this burden:

What makes the death of a parent so much different from other losses?

Why do you think losing a sibling is so difficult for the surviving brothers and sisters?

What are some of the unique sorrows survivors of suicide endure?

Quick access to the book is available at the link below. Enter the link or use your smartphone camera to scan the QRC.

https://amazon.com/dp/B09SL7MYW5

National Tragedy (page 167)

Can you give an example of a national tragedy that brought grief to people who may not have lost someone they knew?

The Covid-19 Pandemic wrought incalculable pain and suffering throughout the world. What are some circumstances that amplified this grief?

Alzheimer's, dementia, and other diseases steal the essence of those that we love little by little, while leaving their bodies behind. How is this grief different?

Types of Grief (page 175)

What are the three major categories of grief?

1)

2)

3)

Briefly, in your own words, describe acute grief.

What is complicated grief?

Describe integrated grief

If you had to identify your grief as one of the three, which would it be and why?

Conclusion (page 185)

Reflections

How has your journey with grief been unique to you alone?

What are your greatest struggles with this beast called grief?

Have you come to that uneasy truce with grief that will allow you to live with this burden?

If you are not at that point in your journey, can you envision such a day?

From everything you have experienced, and learned, about grief, what would be the single most helpful nugget of truth you would want to pass along to your fellow grievers?

Congratulations!

If you have come this far, then you have done the hard work of understanding the enemy that is called grief. You might even understand yourself just a bit better.

Keep this workbook. Refer to it from time to time. You might be amazed by how far you have come.

Your grief may never fully let go, but you will have the victory!

Always Remember the secret to helping yourself is to help others.

Please help others, by leaving a review

"If you found the workbook helpful, it would be greatly appreciated if you left a review so others can receive the same benefits you have. Your review will help us see what is and isn't working, so we can better serve you and all our other readers even more."

Use the QRC or Link below. **https://snip.ly/o7nsfi**

Grief

It's **NOT** Supposed To Be OK!

30-Day Self-Care Guide & Journal

Boost your self-worth & confidence to live a life that is authentic to you.

www.the-grieving-journy.com

Ron Skinner & Jeff Kirk

Hello,

Self-care brings you peace and the confidence to live in alignment with what is best for you. Many of us quickly show love and compassion to others but are hard on ourselves. Our mission is to expand your self-worth, and it starts with this self-care guide.

For the next 30 days, it will prompt you with one self-care action per day. If you feel called to do so, you may rearrange the order of the 30 self-care actions. At the end of 30 days, you will have a clear idea of self-caring actions you may wish to continue for months ahead.

Starting new habits and changing your way of life is not always easy. We are here to affirm that you are free to postpone or even skip activities that do not resonate with you at this moment. But please try.

We are honored to go through this fulfilling self-care journey with you. We wish you all the best.

Ron & Jeff

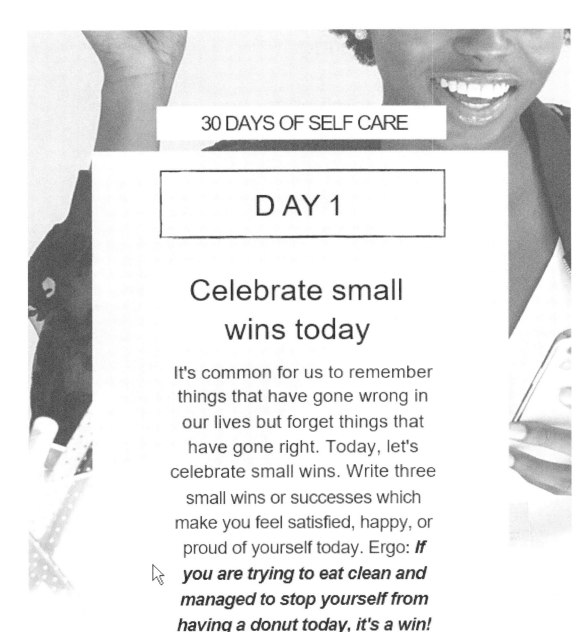

30 DAYS OF SELF CARE

DAY 1

Celebrate small wins today

It's common for us to remember things that have gone wrong in our lives but forget things that have gone right. Today, let's celebrate small wins. Write three small wins or successes which make you feel satisfied, happy, or proud of yourself today. Ergo: *If you are trying to eat clean and managed to stop yourself from having a donut today, it's a win!*

www.the-grieving-journy.com

Five Minute Journaling

One thing I want to remember about today is:

Today I felt …

Today I am grateful for …

D AY 2

Forgive and be kind to yourself

We can be kind to other people but very hard on ourselves. Have you done something which you are not at peace with? Be compassionate with yourself about it. Dig deep and ask: *Why did I do 'that' in the first place? Was I driven by fear, anxiety, or lack of knowledge? If my kids did the same thing, what would I do to be understanding towards them?*

www.the-grieving-journy.com

Five Minute Journaling

One thing I want to remember about today is:

Today I felt …

Today I am grateful for …

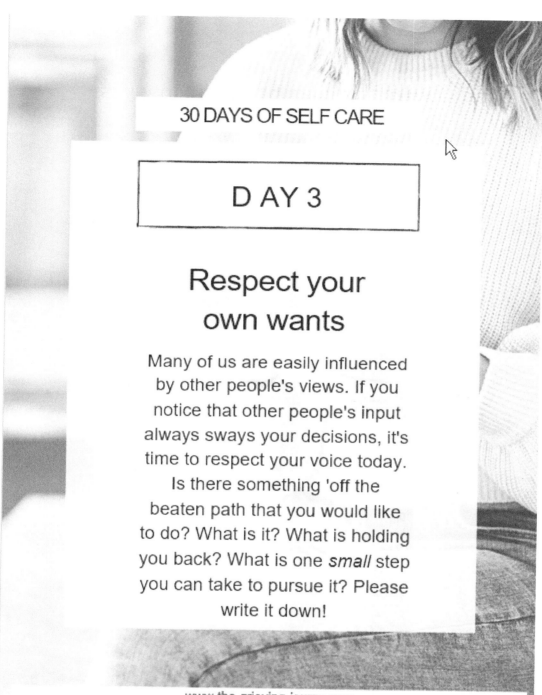

D AY 3

Respect your own wants

Many of us are easily influenced by other people's views. If you notice that other people's input always sways your decisions, it's time to respect your voice today. Is there something 'off the beaten path that you would like to do? What is it? What is holding you back? What is one *small* step you can take to pursue it? Please write it down!

www.the-grieving-journy.com

61

Five Minute Journaling

One thing I want to remember about today is:

Today I felt …

Today I am grateful for …

DAY 4

Start changing an unhelpful belief

Changing beliefs takes time because they have been ingrained in us for decades. You can start by identifying one core negative belief that you want to change. Next, find evidence to 'shoot holes' and disprove this negative belief. This helps you to start questioning if your unhelpful belief is true!

www.the-grieving-journy.com

Five Minute Journaling

One thing I want to remember about today is:

Today I felt …

Today I am grateful for …

30 DAYS OF SELF CARE

D AY 5

Choose positive thoughts & feel good

Positive thoughts are thoughts that support you and your goals. Choose thoughts that make you feel good. Use your feelings as a compass - if you feel upbeat and optimistic, you have positive thoughts in your mind. Your task Today is to make yourself feel good as much as you can.

www.the-grieving-journy.com

Five Minute Journaling

One thing I want to remember about today is:

Today I felt …

Today I am grateful for …

30 DAYS OF SELF CARE

DAY 6

Slow your thought and focus on quieting the storm.

Close your eyes and focus on peaceful thoughts. Engage in all of your five senses where possible. Do this for at least 2 minutes (or longer). Visualizations have to bring up feelings of excitement, abundance, confidence, and other feel-good emotions. Once you feel satisfied, you can stop and visualize again tomorrow if you wish!

www.the-grieving-journy.com

Five Minute Journaling

One thing I want to remember about today is:

Today I felt …

Today I am grateful for …

D AY 7

Take the day off - it's okay to be 'unproductive'

Our modern society fears being 'unproductive.' However, when we take time to smell the roses, we are doing inner work & enriching our mind & soul. I suggest you take the day off from your everyday responsibilities. You may need to plan ahead if you have small kids but do the best you can. A more refreshed 'you' awaits.

www.the-grieving-journy.com

Five Minute Journaling

One thing I want to remember about today is:

Today I felt …

Today I am grateful for …

D AY 8

Eat mindfully &
enjoy your meal more

Today, we shall eat mindfully with no distractions. Place your phone, laptop, books, and tech devices away. Enjoy the meal in front of you. Pick a dish you enjoy eating and savor every morsel and appreciate the effort it takes for the chef (or someone else) to prepare the meal. Enjoy and be mindful of the sights and sounds around you, too.

Five Minute Journaling

One thing I want to remember about today is:

Today I felt …

Today I am grateful for …

D AY 9

Take an online class you enjoy for the fun of it

For today, let's take an online class (free or paid) on a non-work-related topic you enjoy. Perhaps you enjoy writing fiction, digital drawing, cooking, fashion...etc. Go on YouTube or even pay for a class if you wish. Indulge in a topic you enjoy just for the sheer joy of it.

www.the-grieving-journy.com

Five Minute Journaling

One thing I want to remember about today is:

Today I felt …

Today I am grateful for …

DAY 1 0

Do a tech detox & enjoy your day more

A 'tech detox' may be a pleasant experience. Today, vow only to check your mobile phone once an hour: a glance at your notifications for messages or emails every hour. After a few minutes of scrolling, put down your phone and occupy yourself with other activities. Lastly, 1 hour before bedtime, switch off your laptops, phones, and tech devices & you may enjoy better sleep!

www.the-grieving-journy.com

Five Minute Journaling

One thing I want to remember about today is:

Today I felt …

Today I am grateful for …

30 DAYS OF SELF CARE

DAY 1 1

Plan for a gossip-free day

Gossiping can be a guilty pleasure. It can make us feel more superior or 'better' than others. Today, spare yourself from this practice of talking ill of others. Respect yourself and choose not to partake in this activity today. If you are caught in the middle of a gossiping session, change the subject or excuse yourself gracefully from the group.

www.the-grieving-journy.com

Five Minute Journaling

One thing I want to remember about today is:

Today I felt …

Today I am grateful for …

30 DAYS OF SELF CARE

DAY 1 1

Plan for a gossip-free day

Gossiping can be a guilty pleasure. It can make us feel more superior or 'better' than others. Today, spare yourself from this practice of talking ill of others. Respect yourself and choose not to partake in this activity today. If you are caught in the middle of a gossiping session, change the subject or excuse yourself gracefully from the group.

Five Minute Journaling

One thing I want to remember about today is:

Today I felt …

Today I am grateful for …

DAY 1 3

Listen to
mindset-altering tunes

Listen to some binaural beats today. Binaural beats can alter the state of your mind to be more alert, positive, or more relaxed. There are thousands of free binaural beats available on YouTube. These tunes are usually hours long, but you can stop when you feel satisfied. Choose one binaural beat tune from YouTube and see if it makes a difference to how you feel!

www.the-grieving-journy.com

Five Minute Journaling

One thing I want to remember about today is:

Today I felt …

Today I am grateful for …

DAY 1 4

Do 1thing you have been procrastinating on

Is there a task or chore that you have been putting off *forever*? Today we are going to tackle this one task. Choose a task that has been bothering you, and you can complete it today. Be sure to pick a task that will make you feel satisfied or relieved once it's done! If you have the energy, pick more than 1 task today.

www.the-grieving-journy.com

Five Minute Journaling

One thing I want to remember about today is:

Today I felt …

Today I am grateful for …

DAY 1 5

Create an exciting goal to empower yourself

Nothing makes a goal more natural than writing it down. I'm sure there is at least ONE thing you are burning to achieve by the end of this year or within these few months. What is it? Your goal has to bring up feelings of excitement within you. At the same time, it has to be *believable* to you. Write down one exciting and believable goal to work on.

www.the-grieving-journy.com

Five Minute Journaling

One thing I want to remember about today is:

Today I felt …

Today I am grateful for …

DAY 1 6

Say good things only!

Positive words hold positive energy. Today, try as much as you can only to say positive things. Instead of looking at a handbag and saying, "*I can't afford this*," say, "I will buy this in the future if I still like it then!" Instead of "*Why do I always make mistakes at work?*", say, "I'm still learning." You get the idea!

www.the-grieving-journy.com

Five Minute Journaling

One thing I want to remember about today is:

Today I felt …

Today I am grateful for …

DAY 1 7

Create a life-changing affirmation

Affirmations work because when you tell yourself something repeatedly, your subconscious mind starts to believe it. Create an affirmation that feels good and specific to you. It's best to say the affirmation to yourself during high-vibe moments in the day when you feel upbeat and optimistic. Practice this for 30 days (or more)!

www.the-grieving-journy.com

Five Minute Journaling

One thing I want to remember about today is:

Today I felt …

Today I am grateful for …

DAY 1 8

Celebrate your inner beauty

You possess beautiful qualities which can create positive change. What are those qualities? Jot down at least 10 of those beautiful qualities that you have. *Write spontaneously without censoring yourself and keep this list private if you wish.* What can you do to enhance and use these ten life-changing qualities to benefit the world or people around you?

www.the-grieving-journy.com

Five Minute Journaling

One thing I want to remember about today is:

Today I felt …

Today I am grateful for …

DAY 1 9

Start finding your higher purpose

We are all created with a unique mix of gifts, talents, and shortcomings. All of us have a part to play in this world. To have a sense of your higher purpose, ponder which activities bring you joy. Your higher purpose is linked to your joy. Write down three activities that bring you joy and can positively change society or the world.

www.the-grieving-journy.com

Five Minute Journaling

One thing I want to remember about today is:

Today I felt …

Today I am grateful for …

DAY 2 0

Stop comparing yourself today

If your friends are in high-earning jobs and you are not, it's hard not to feel your stomach clench when they talk of their essential job scopes and shopping sprees. Is there an area in life where you constantly compare yourself against other people? Does this mean you want more of *'that thing'* in your life? What can you do to get *'that thing'*? Brainstorm your ideas and write them down.

www.the-grieving-journy.com

95

Five Minute Journaling

One thing I want to remember about today is:

Today I felt …

Today I am grateful for …

DAY 2 1

3 things you love about your physical beauty

Is there something you appreciate about your physical beauty? Your expressive eyes, your clear skin, or perhaps your genuine smile? If you look hard enough, you can find 3-5 areas of your body that you love. Please take note of them and appreciate your physical beauty today (in fact, every day!).

www.the-grieving-journy.com

Five Minute Journaling

One thing I want to remember about today is:

Today I felt …

Today I am grateful for …

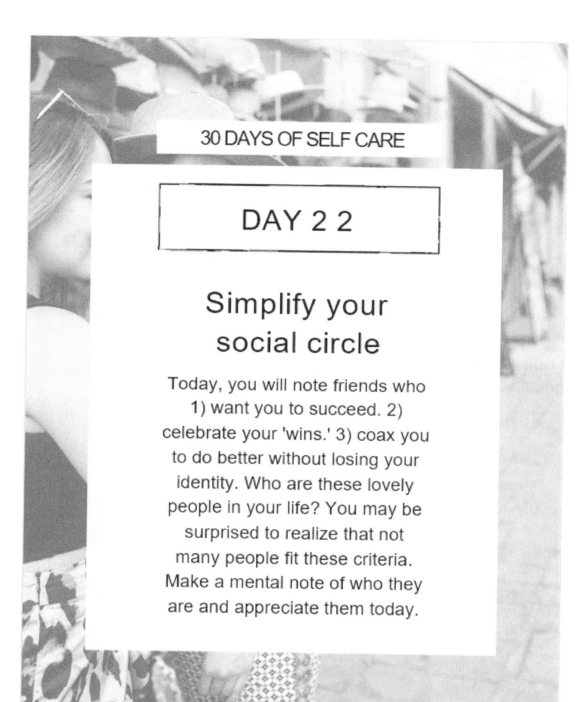

DAY 2 2

Simplify your social circle

Today, you will note friends who 1) want you to succeed. 2) celebrate your 'wins.' 3) coax you to do better without losing your identity. Who are these lovely people in your life? You may be surprised to realize that not many people fit these criteria. Make a mental note of who they are and appreciate them today.

www.the-grieving-journy.com

Five Minute Journaling

One thing I want to remember about today is:

Today I felt …

Today I am grateful for …

DAY 2 3

Say 'No' and set healthy boundaries

Is there something you keep doing even though you hate doing it? Strategize how you can say 'no' to such activities politely. Or arrange for alternatives to make those disliked activities more likable. If you suspect that someone is taking advantage of your kindness, today is time to plan how to say 'no' without hurting the relationship.

Five Minute Journaling

One thing I want to remember about today is:

Today I felt …

Today I am grateful for …

DAY 2 4

Meditate to reduce overthinking

Meditating helps to keep your thoughts under control. It calms you, gives you perspective, and makes you feel more alert. You can get wonderful guided meditations for free on YouTube. Set aside time to meditate for as long as you like today. *Pro-tip: choose a guided meditation that you feel particularly drawn to.*

www.the-grieving-journy.com

Five Minute Journaling

One thing I want to remember about today is:

Today I felt …

Today I am grateful for …

DAY 2 5

Practice being present

The present moment is all we
have right now. Instead of
looking forward to the future,
how about being thankful for the
beauty of 'right now?' You can
also be present while washing
the dishes, meditating,
journaling, or doing enjoyable
activities which do not require
tech devices. Being present helps
you make good decisions every
day.

www.the-grieving-journy.com

Five Minute Journaling

One thing I want to remember about today is:

Today I felt …

Today I am grateful for …

DAY 2 6

Change your negative thoughts

This is easier said than done, but you can start small today. Pinpoint one negative thought that you want to change. Challenge it. Ask yourself, "Is this thought 100% true? Can I list some evidence that proves that this thought is NOT true? Can I create a new, more positive thought to replace this unhelpful thought?"

www.the-grieving-journy.com

Five Minute Journaling

One thing I want to remember about today is:

Today I felt …

Today I am grateful for …

DAY 2 7

Eat 1 healthy meal today

Suppose you are consistent about clean eating. Good for you! If you need help in this area, you can start eating one healthy meal a day. Choose clean, wholesome food which is the least processed. If you are ready to make this an everyday habit, you will feel more alert and energized in your day-to-day life.

www.the-grieving-journy.com

Five Minute Journaling

One thing I want to remember about today is:

Today I felt …

Today I am grateful for …

DAY 2 8

30 Minutes of 'Me-time'

When you spend time in solitude, your best ideas and solutions come to mind. Allocate 30-60 minutes of solitude time today. Take a long walk, sit in a park or spend time with yourself alone at home. One rule: you have to be free of tech devices. You will notice solutions to problems or inspired actions pop into your mind.

www.the-grieving-journy.com

Five Minute Journaling

One thing I want to remember about today is:

Today I felt …

Today I am grateful for …

DAY 2 9

Be with
positive people

Think of 3 people in your life who lift your mood, make you feel inspired, and are supportive of your endeavors. Consciously plan to meet or communicate with them more often. Schedule a coffee meetup or chat with one of them today.

www.the-grieving-journy.com

Five Minute Journaling

One thing I want to remember about today is:

Today I felt …

Today I am grateful for …

DAY 3 0

Get inspired!

Today is time for you to feel optimistic and inspired about your goals. Choose an uplifting podcast or audiobook to listen to. Read motivating articles or stream motivating videos on YouTube if you prefer visuals. It is best if you can make this a daily habit! Set aside 30-60 minutes to get inspired every day.

www.the-grieving-journy.com

Five Minute Journaling

One thing I want to remember about today is:

Today I felt …

Today I am grateful for …

We want to share more advice to help you

be more confident and self-caring.

Join our exclusive Facebook Group where you can share,
find comfort, and comfort others:

SCAN HERE

to be in our Facebook Group

Please help others find the help they need by leaving a review.

"If you found the workbook helpful, it would be greatly appreciated if you left a review so others can receive the same benefits you have. Your review will help us see what is and isn't working, so we can better serve you and all our other readers even more."

Use the QRC or Link below.

https://snip.ly/o7nsfi

Made in the USA
Las Vegas, NV
19 July 2024

92603689R00066